Veil Of Emotions

Aching Chunks of My Anatomy Vol. 1

Abhinav Makker

BookLeaf
Publishing

India | USA | UK

Dedication

This book is dedicated to the strongest and most unwavering support systems in my life—my ever-loving and selfless parents Mr. Ramesh Kumar Makker ji and Mrs. Mantosh Makker ji, my compassionate and inspiring brother - Abhishek and his wife Vaishali; my deeply caring and understanding wife - Shefali, and irreplaceable family and friends. Your unconditional love and constant encouragement have been the pillars of my strength. I also want to extend my boundless love to delightful and radiant niece, Aashvi, and cheerful nephew, Aarav.

This book is also dedicated to the lost but eternally cherished souls who remain alive in my heart—my deeply missed grandparents, kind-hearted cousin Aakash, best friend Ashwin, and legendary singer, Chester B. Your memories continue to guide and uplift me in ways words can never truly express.

You are all an everlasting part of this journey.

Preface

Poetry has always been a mirror—sometimes reflecting
what we choose to see, other times revealing what we
try to hide. This book is a collection of those reflections—
of thoughts that whisper in the quiet, emotions that
refuse to be silenced, and wounds that speak in verses.

Each poem in these pages comes from a place of deep
feeling, whether it's the weight of loss, the quiet battle of
the mind, the longing for something lost, or the strength
found in survival. Some pieces are raw, some gentle,
some unsettling, and some comforting. But all of them
are real.

I did not write these poems to provide answers. I wrote
them to be felt—to be understood by those who have
known pain, love, uncertainty, and hope. If even one line
in this book makes you pause, makes you see yourself, or
makes you feel less alone, then this collection has done
its job.

This book is for you—the overthinker, the quiet sufferer,
the fighter, the dreamer, and the one searching for
meaning in chaos. Whatever brought you here, I hope
these words keep you company.

Acknowledgements

No journey is ever walked alone, and this book would not have been possible without the love, support, and encouragement of those who have stood by me.

To my family, your belief in me has been my greatest strength. Your patience, understanding, and support have given me the space to create, and for that, I am endlessly grateful. This book carries pieces of my heart, but so many of those pieces belong to you.

To my closest friends, thank you for always being there —not just in moments of celebration, but in the quiet struggles too. Your words, laughter, and presence have shaped me in more ways than I can express. A special mention - Atif for reviewing book thoroughly.

And to everyone who has ever listened, encouraged, or simply understood—thank you. This book is as much yours as it is mine.

Special thanks to Jonathan Cooper for the front cover, available via Pexels.

1. Journalism's journey to death

The stakeholders pets and puppets you, so accordingly the headlines align.
We know that you run shows and ruin fellows in prime time at nine.
Your net-worth jumped, with millions of bucks pumped, in your backyard,
Yet, strangely, you still are unaffordable to buy or even borrow a moral spine.
Ironically, with all the seriousness, you call yourself an "ideal" journalist,
by hiding facts and only unveiling dictated, guttered-glitters that shine.

You deliberately manufacture stuff, funnelling through your propagandist verdicts.
As you have decayed, you hold decades of experience in the art of "How to malign?".
The underprivileged are doomed, marooned, abandoned, they die in neglect,
When you and your hefty-pocketed corporate pals cling to glasses of wine.
Yet another abiding blow on the already weakening social fabric,

And yet another innocent being bothered, butchered,
thronged like swine.

Your cunning skills earned culinary breads to you while
leaving us with piles of fleshless bones.
As the hatred you spewed, you irresponsibly brewed,
while sipping coffee in studio online.
It reaped rewards to you, seeping into all municipality
wards, but it ripped families apart,
As shrewdly stewarded by you in the name of the holy -
the divine shrine.
Fatherless children sit clueless, helpless in the grieving
hour, devastated,
While you shove the mic to their mouths like regular,
heartless, divisive design.

Lunatic, pathetic, preposterous, stooped, crooked,
corrupted, apocalyptic are you,
As the numbers that mattered plummet, while your
nurtured hatred numbers incline.
You iteratively assaulted and ruptured the soul of the
nation, including mine.
You, a disgrace, a menace to the country and to your
own professional line,
Your tethered spirit that you sold in ounces now
congregates with us and whines.

The world damningly knows that, you run shows and ruin fellows in your prime time at nine.

2. The serpent: so-called journalist

You fool, adding fuel, wrongly school billion fellow
citizens every day.
With zero shame, wicked games—still, you seek fresh,
deceptive ways.
Your long-diminished morality, has now completely
swayed.
Your propaganda drives countrymen to drag each other's
lives into an ashtray.
You could have been responsible, sensible, but chose to
be terrible right away.
The real issues the country is concerned with—you park
them cleverly at bay.

Following directions from your minister-master, you
daily swing foul play.
Because you wilfully dump and slump matters into
shades of murkier grey,
You can never be the light; you can never be the
goddamn enlightening ray,
You throw away the matters knowingly —the matters
that genuinely weigh.
You—your lord's servant, a poisonous serpent—lust for
TRPs shows you the way.

You draft and craft vandalism—for which you get paid,
but the country-fellows pay.

You, ruthless, heartless, soulless—nothing but a
controlled meagre lump of clay.
You, lunatic, you, pathetic, now the nation knows and
they have a lot to say.
May it bothers you, smother you—may you never forget,
but regret it in utter dismay!
May you ponder the blunders, and finally surrender to
the torturous thought's array.
May it jolt you, haunt you, and daunt you—until you can
no longer stay,
Until you collapse beneath the weight of your own
decay; beneath the weight of your own decay.

3. It is easier to kill humans than to kill their nightmare

Engulfing each and every longitude and latitude,
Across all the behaviors and varied attitudes,
Hatred spread so vast, for years and years it last,
Systematically it murdered six million in the Holocaust.
Before the gassing; ornaments, watches, and women
were looted.
In a matter of minutes, hundreds of victims were
shockingly muted.
Round the clock, this ruthless act continued and geared.
It is easier to collectively kill humans than to kill their
nightmare.

The army of the Japanese was brutal; thus, they met the
same unfortunate fate.
Two atomic attacks completely changed the course of the
war and the state.
Just two cities—thousands of civilian killings were
unjustifiably justified,
Yet, even decades later, justice remains file-buried and
crucified.
Handicapped, mutated, and malformed, born to this day
in bombed cities,
the scientifically advancements swiftly bring us to dooms

day's proximity.
Though their own countrymen opposed the bombings,
still, a leader dared.
It is easier to collectively kill humans than to kill their
nightmare.

The distant southeast witnessed the greatest mass
displacement.
As two nations were born free from the royal kingdom's
enslavement.
In Bengal famine, vultures circled above the dying
bodies, starving dogs waited beside;
As tons of wheat for world-war was diverted, so four
million fell to callous "colonial genocide".
Fourteen million migrated at the brink of freedom,
prosperity and blood-thirst knives;
In the crazy chaos, in the blooded brotherhood, around
two million lost their lives.
Loots, scattered boots, red drapes, rapes and not to forget
Jallianwala Bagh massacre.
It is easier to collectively kill humans than to kill their
nightmare.

In the name of God, the mother Earth has seen and
soaked enough blood.
For God's sake, enough is enough, end this relentless
outrageous flood!

This madhouse depends on the one who sits in the most
powerful of the chairs.
Humans acting inhumane everywhere, acts of humanity,
a sight very rare.
Injustice wreaking havoc, demands for justice runs in
newspapers and prayers.
The mortals are all gone; only their souls remain
complaining in the air.
Even the almighty, with all his might, each and every
time, silently stares.
It is easier to collectively kill humans than to kill their
nightmare.

4. My happy time

You are my first rhyme, my happy time.
You are my prime, my partner in crime.
The soothing sounds of a wind chime.

You are my autumn's breeze, my pizza's cheese.
You are my eternal peace, my vacationing at Greece.
The rush of joy my heart can't cease.

You are my sole sunshine, my silver line.
You are my lone shrine, my divine's sign.
Around you, I orbit by fate's design.

You are my winter's miss, my summer's oasis.
You are my eternal bliss, my forehead kiss.
And as you read this, you know you're part of this.

You are where my heart inclines, where our stars align.
You are the only reason, I keep doing perfectly fine.
Today and always, may our souls intertwine.

5. Just stay

Just stay. Just stay.
Stay with me each hour,
Each day, every day.
Just stay. Just stay.
From the wild winters of December
To the warmth of April and May.
Just stay. Just stay.
From the darkest of the nights,
To the light-pouring day.
Just stay. Just stay.
It's gloomy; do not go away.
You, the spark; you, the only ray.
Just stay. Just stay.
It's not me, it's not you—
It's us, always, all the way.
Just stay. Just stay.

6. I feel

How does a bird feel without wings?
How does a kingdom feel without a king?
I feel the same without you.

How does an ocean feel without waves?
How does an army feel without braves?
I feel the same without you.

How does the rainbow look without colors?
How does a perfume smells without odour?
I feel the same without you.

How does a sunflower feel without sun?
How does a human feel without oxygen?
I feel the same without you.

7. Flesh trade

Marks of oppression, embossed on her heart, skin, and brain,
Her shivering body was engulfed in her shrieking, shooting pain.
She was bruised, bloodied, burnt—canine-eaten, with a bitten lip.
Her fears, insecurities, and anxieties—all at once, unzipped.

Parts of her body were burnt—her body was compellingly governed.
Her freedom, her chills, her screams—all boisterously governed.
Penetrated, violated—deeper the clenching wild nails,
Only the wall could lend an ear to her flinching tragic tale.

Consciously-naked men in sinister streets openly parade;
seeking, scouring murky markets for fresh flesh to trade.
There, she was trapped, slapped, dragged, drugged, and abused.
Her muscles, tissues, soul, her strength strangled—alas, none accused.

Brittle bones, broken spirit, - her belly, like humanity,
starved.
In unknown numbers missing—today, another angel's
life cruelly carved.
As she crawled; the omnipotent lord did not save her
from heinous crimes.
When she was mauled, god's men and men's god did not
save her million times.

8. Subject

Medical subject is sent for terrifying tests, sustaining serious injury.
Protests arise from the masses and media; soon joins the film industry.
An inquiry is launched by the Women's Welfare Ministry.
A court case proceeds, overseen by the honorary judiciary.
Acquitted or convicted, the accused is sent to psychiatry by the jury.

Because the accused, burdened with allegations, is a minor—a juvenile.
With the traits of a reptile and the tears of a crocodile's guile.
Yet, he knows, the case will be tossed into bureaucracy's pile.
Such cases had been repeated countless times, in history,
With past references pulled, as judges draw symmetry.

While evil reigns and prevails, driven by lust-filled deeds,
Blood from ruptured, punctured, and battered bodies bleeds.

As the flaws in the laws spread like weeds, justice
recedes.
Blood and relations bear stains of horror and misery,
While justice rooms churn out nothing but mockery.

9. Biography of a cancer warrior

Lying, trying, but dying in the hospital bed,
with no hair on the body and the stitched head.
My body fails to endure the endless therapy sessions.
I have left behind my routine, my dreams, my passions.
When the world peacefully sleeps, piece by piece, I
decay.
How much longer can my strength keep fate at bay?

I am fed up, looking up for a reliving break.
A holiday escape, a movie, a piece of cake?
I am in a constant battle that too with my own self.
Some terrifying thoughts rattle me under the shelf.
I see you, watching and trying hard to holdback a tear.
At worst, I fight the urge to burst, forcing on a cheer.

I feel, I am prepared to take the final call.
This continuous fight feels like a snowball.
It has taken a toll now winning feels like a fall.
I have run out of my strength to dangle and cling.
It's time for the angels to descend and sing.
It's time for the angels to descend and sing.

10. Ashes

Stood dozen, her body frozen—the sons lights up the ashes.
Few think of all her phases, her phrases as her memory flashes.
A human before last breath, now a body; in flames, she dresses.
Never going to blink those beautiful long-curled eyelashes.
They shared childhood also together, but now, sibling clashes.

Heating up the air, angry fire from the pyre splashes,
As she departs, they talk property, and hidden stashes.
Nobody wants the hoards of her smiling canvases.
People take sides; the grave issue, nobody addresses.
She left her name, pains, and relations—as she goes up in gases.

She goes up in gases..

11. Requiem

Committed thousands of sins and crimes,
Oh, heartless time—you have done it countless times.
You were as brutal as you could be; you are cruel,
You don't use our emotions as your fuel.
Time, you run carefree and ceaseless;
You won't stop— you are shameless!

I begged, I pleaded only if you could hear,
To turn around the time, to bring them near.
So we could meet and greet our dear ones,
Reliving thousand moments in just one.
Hard and harsh reality is hollow - just a void,
Unaware of different means to be destroyed.

Time is utterly powerful, and we, bitterly weak,
It bends us, breaks us, twists us in streak.
We never knew that the glance was the last,
Still bleeding from the wounds of the past.
And now, haunted by a lingering ghost,
We ache, we long - we love you the most!

12. You were there

When I was stressed,
When I was suppressed,
You were there beside me.
When I could not figure things out,
When I could not set plans in route,
You were there beside me.

When I was shattered,
When I was battered,
You were there beside me.
When I was in anger,
When I stood stronger,
You were there beside me.

When I had good rhymes,
When I had bad times,
You were there beside me.
When people left, you managed to stay.
When I learned lessons the hard way,
You were there beside me.

How did you defy this universal law—
Of fleeing at the first heavy blow?
You were there beside me.

I always wished, and we stayed together.
Fortunate, to have a friend through all weathers.
You are still there beside me!

13. In my bed

Crushed, crunched, drenched in my pillow.
Feeling so low from my head to toe.
What shall I provide as the reason for this fever?
My heart breaks, bones ache, body shivers.

I pull myself up from this lonely, cold bed.
My dark circles speak my story with eyes red.
Thoughts running deep, I wish I could get some more
sleep.
With moving week, growing weak, the alarm beeps,
sorrow seeps.

Looking in the closet for a shirt and rugged jeans.
I push myself through my monotonous daily routines.
Trying to keep myself buoyant, trying to keep sane.
Finally, I head back into the wild and unavoidable lane.

14. Unjustifiably taxed

Pressure, fever, suppression,
Ruins and sufferings in my body.
Why is this not taxed?

Fears, failures, aches abandon,
Unexpressed worries in my body.
Why is this not taxed?

Imperfections, infections, polluted oxygen,
Microplastics, sugar cravings in my body.
Why is this not taxed?

The lost ones, the longing ones,
The missed opportunities in my body.
Why is this not taxed?

Fate hurls us into the untamed unknown.
Peace never dwells in a crumbling body.
Why is this not taxed?

15. Fighter

They talk about your fall, but you'll be the last man standing.
Even if you must crawl, still refuse to crash landing.
Be ready to take every punch straight to the face,
Stand tall like a fortress, unshaken in place.

Oh, can't see the light at the end of the tunnel?
Then you be the legend etched in historic annals.
Are you ready to deliver the toughest of tests?
Are you ready to register a power-packed protest?

Then, with an iron will, march ahead to the triumphant drums.
Sitting on a king's throne, spit their opinions —like bubble gum.
You are the son of the burning sun, the jungle's roaring king.
Now the universe bows before you — master, the fighter in the ring!

16. You are a star with scars

Believe me, you are doing fine.
You fell eight, but you got up nine.
Took hundreds head-on, not with a brittle spine.
Do not stop here after getting this far.
It's just another scar on a bright star.

A thousand battles you have bravely fought.
Your proven mettle isn't meant to rot.
You are certainly more than you had thought.
This is just another closure of another war.
It's just another scar on a bright star.

You are made of surreal cosmic stuff.
You are ruthless and banging tough.
Great sailors are defined by paths rough.
You are soon going to raise the bar.
It's just another scar on a bright star.

17. I am a riot

Sitting, under the shadow of trees with dancing breeze.
Settling in my me-time—unsettling talks? DND, please!
My heart should be put to asylum, my brain appears
numb.
At this hour, shifting states kills me whole—my inner
succumbs.

Compelling, propelling, shelling train of thoughts under
my shell.
Squeezing in, zoning out—what is happening? I am
unable to tell.

In the day, my mind wanders—I aimlessly doodle.
At night, how to get rid of this situation, I Google.
Lost in endless stories, wandering from app to app,
Tired, but tirelessly swiping from Insta to Whatsapp.

Do you do the same? Are we in the same boat?
Do you feel the same, though maybe we never spoke?

Peep in my heart's window to see the tethering,
torturing tornado.
Appear same in day, sane in day—then submit to night's
shadow.

I am a vessel comprising stress and carelessness.
If the layers undress, I am an unheard herd's mess.

I guess I gotta run, yes, I gotta run.
My roaring, tearing silences need to shun.
I insist—it spares none, hence I gotta run.
The gods, the stalwarts—I am gonna summon.
Light is for few, fight is for everyone.
Light is for few, but others remain in dungeon.
I gotta run, I gotta run.

I am a riot—twenty thoughts, all rotten.
A riot of echoes, of scars unforgotten.

18. Wolf in sheep

In the middle of an oceanic hustle,
I take beatings from a ruthless tussle,
The kind that is silent yet strong,
Unseen, but carrying me along.

Meanwhile,
Social media keeps opening new jars,
Feeding the inner fight, gaslighting unseen wars.
But you need to get up, kick off your woes,
Go, arm yourself, get back on your toes.

Face the problem - no forced grin,
Turn the struggle to strength within.
When the rest sleep, stop your weeps,
Unleash the wolf from the skin of the sheep.

19. Mental health : An important issue

I know that there are hidden, down-trodden wars;
I know that there are forbidden, unridden scars.
If not fiercely fought, they will eat you;
they will kick you down, they will beat, retreat you.

Forgive yourself, you have to get rid of all sort of
thoughts.
They grow terrible, troubling when left to rot.
Fight every night, with thousands of them, but don't
surrender.
Show them the real you, don't let them steal your
thunder.
When it bothers, reach out to others, but do not fall
weak.
Voyage out, vent out, we are here to listen, not critique

UN reports claim mental disorders in people, one out of
four.
The conditions occupied significant space and now
openly roar.
Many to name— anxiety, depression, bipolar disorders;
with it billions of people are affected across the borders.
Hence, it is proven to be a hefty wealth;

taking care of your physical as well as mental health.

They shocked the near ones sitting beside;
Avicii, Chester similarly many, had too little to decide.
So hear me now—your presence matters!
For the nearest ones, your essence matters.
While silently tears might be wiped with a tissue,
Let's say it aloud—mental health is an issue!

20. When I die

I won't lie, but when I die, I won't actually die.
I'll live in the hearts of friends and family nearby.
I'll donate all my organs—every part that could be,
So next time you see someone, it could be parts of me.
Bury my remnants, let me nourish the earth beneath;
I'll be around when you need—the oxygen you breathe.

I'll pour my essence into trees, bees, and beans,
Finding my way back to you through different means.
Perhaps, I'll be the force that helps a seed germinate,
Or the energy in a singing bird on an evening late.
While I decay, while I daily decompose, still, I'll be close.
I might bloom in your garden as your next blossoming
rose.

After I am underneath and while eyes well;
I won't depart to imaginary heavens or hells.
I'll have signed off from the world's wicked games,
Yet remain alive in photographs and frames.
In memories, they'll look for me in the sky as stars.
We are stellar outcomes, yet not destined so far.

Some will remember me for the person I was since birth,
Others might recall me by my deeds and my worth.

I'll leave behind fewer aching chunks of my anatomy,
And set myself free—onto my next earthly journey.
So, when I die, I'll live on in varied forms—I won't
actually die.
I'll transform, evolve, and support life after my final
goodbye.

21. Queries and curiosity

In the colossal cosmos, spanning beyond imagination,
universes hold galaxies in billions.
Each galaxy further has planets in billions—what are the
odds of thriving life? One in a zillion?
With a million species here, one being sapiens, I am one
among 800 crore human companions.
A fact: our bodies share the same elements, similar
fundamental representations.
*"The nitrogen in our DNA, the calcium in our teeth, the
iron in our blood, the carbon*
*in our apple pies were made in the interiors of collapsing
stars. We are made of star stuff,"*
as factually claimed by the veteran astronomer Carl
Sagan.

Theories claim primitive life started near hydrothermal
vents, deep under the oceans.
From single-celled organisms to complex beings,
evolution took its mutations.
Thereafter, they learned replication, migration, and
surviving mass extinctions.
Humans share 98% of their DNA with chimps and
gorillas, 97% with orangutans.
A seed sown by gods or a deliberate act of an intelligent

form of aliens?

All DNA and RNA bases have been discovered in meteorites—isn't this a scientific indication?

From single-celled life to Homo sapiens—is it a tale of evolutionary transformations?

After cognitive evolution, we arrived at the division of nations, bound by cultures and religions.

Stringent laws were brought in to govern and hold accountability of each and every civilian.

Then came the blooming lust for profits, plunders, pogroms, colonization, and annexations.

Oppenheimer rightly quoted, *"Now I have become Death, the destroyer of worlds,"* after the nuclear detonation.

Oh, did we count the development of ballistic missiles and biological weapons in parallel with UN negotiations?

Collaborating in space while declaring wars on each other—the two sides of powerful nations.

Among experiments conducted up there, scientists grew plants and embryos on the International Space Station.

In the 21st century, there are alarming concerns over pollution, recessions, inflations and overpopulation.

Schoolchildren raise awareness, stakeholders fly in personal jet planes for global warming discussions.

Microplastics are discovered in foetuses, human blood,

hearts, lungs, arctic ice, clouds, and oceans.
The rapid mushrooming of urbanization, along with
globalization, digitization, and radicalization.
As chopping heads go hand in hand with head
transplants. Faiths and beliefs govern fates and
conclusions.
Hunger, poverty, national debts rise and social media
reshaping the elections and public opinions.
Meanwhile, Xenobots—robots created from living cells—
are programmed, capable of repair and replication.

The fights, the frictions, targeted expulsions —games of
perception, money, muscle power, and convictions.
"When life leaves us behind, love keeps us kind", sang
the late, legendary singer Chester Bennington.
"Let everyone be one's own. No one should be stranger."
essayed young Bhagat Singh, a revolutionary Indian.
*"You develop an instant global consciousness, a people
orientation, an intense dissatisfaction*
with the state of the world, and a compulsion to do
something about it. From out there on the moon,
international politics looks so petty," quoted Edgar
Mitchell, an astronaut from the Apollo 14 mission.
Meanwhile, an unbothered star in our vicinity burns in
nuclear fusion, sustaining life and vegetation.

Tesla remarked, *"Egos, beliefs, and fear separate us, but*

we are all one."

While contemplating abiogenetic carbon compounds
that created all forms of life—
trees, animals, viruses, and organs—I wonder about the
chemical complexity called creation.
Apparently, a carbon-based form of life, knitted with
consciousness, and emotions.
I ponder the inner and outer worlds. I take a sigh—who
are we? Who am I in this equation?
With my queries and curiosity, I consider, "We could
have been empathetic, still do not consider to be one."
with all the facts, recorded history, research, innovations,
quotations and interlinked "relations".

* 9 7 8 9 3 6 9 5 4 5 9 1 9 *